THE ART OF VIKING COMBAT

M. J. Erbach

Copyright © 2024 M. J. Erbach

All rights reserved

The characters and illustrations portrayed in this book are fictitious. Any similarity to real persons, living or dead, is coincidental and not intended by the illustrator.

No part of this book may be reproduced, or stored in a retrieval system, or transmitted in any form or by any means, electronic, mechanical, photocopying, recording, or otherwise, without express written permission of the publisher.

ISBN: 9798300234010

Cover image: Detail of the Bayeux Tapestry, Scene 58, depiction of warriors with Skjoldr and Swords, as well as Long Axes

Printed in the United States of America

This work is dedicated to Loch, Dane, Raven, and all of the other friends and opponents who have helped inform this study. Well met, Well fought.
All proceeds from the sale of this book go to support the Warriors of Ash School of the Blade, a 501(c)3 non-profit educational organization.

CONTENTS

Title Page
Copyright
Dedication
Introduction: What This Is and Is Not   1
Chapter 1: The Long Axe or Skeggox   7
Chapter 2: The Viking Shield, or Skjoldr   17
Chapter 3: Dual Weilding Hand Axe and Sword   35
Chapter 4: Team Combat   42
Chapter 5: Fight Strategy and Battle Geometry   48
About The Author   63
Books By This Author   65

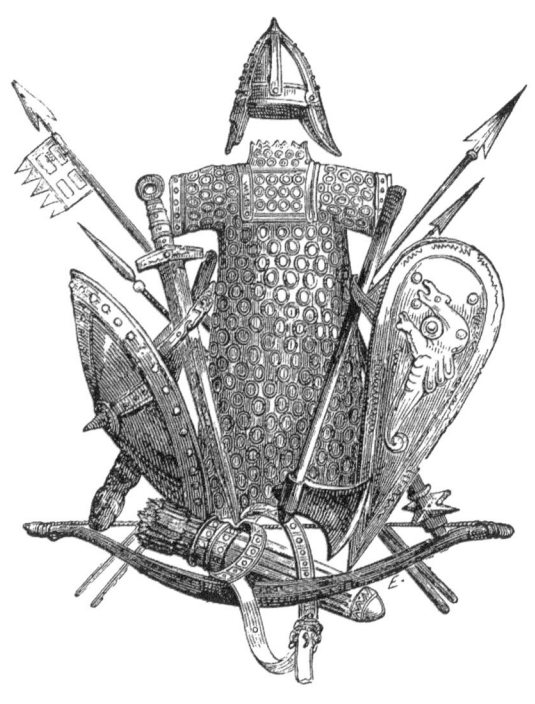

Rendering of a selection of the weapons and armor depicted on the Bayeux Tapestry, used by fighters at the Battle of Hastings, 1066ce

The Art of Viking Combat

By Mike "The Viking" Erbach

Through the application of experimental archaeology, I seek to discover what would have been possible for ancient Scandinavian warriors, commonly now known as "Vikings", diverse and varied as they were, to enact on the differing opponents they faced. The study of archaeological evidence, human biomechanics, and the practical application of historically accurate weapon replicas at full fight speed help inform our understanding of what specific actions would have been useful for Viking warriors in their pursuit of victory at this particular time and place in history.

INTRODUCTION: WHAT THIS IS AND IS NOT

Viking Era Combat Reconstruction, unlike many other historically sourced weapon combat sports, does not exist quite within the realm of Historical European Martial Arts, or HEMA. Its forms and techniques are not drawn from any historical treatise. There are no original manuals that describe with illustration the particulars of the art, which HEMA practitioners are generally so blessed with. IF any of the Scandinavian warriors wrote down any of their techniques, those sources either did not survive or have yet to be discovered. And since there are no manuals, there are no Viking Combat Masters to study. No modern person can say they know "the true art of the Viking warrior". This means that we are now all equal, all students in the pursuit of this obscure knowledge, which we must discover not by studying a book or listening to a teacher, but by doing. It is a living, evolving art, and the best techniques are always proven in the ring.

However, that does not mean that we have no historical sources from which to draw. Visual resources like the Bayeux Tapestry show us what weapons of the time looked like and how they were held. Written accounts like the Anglo-Saxon Chronicle, the journals of Ibn Fadlan, and the histories of Venerable Bede describe in detail what these outsiders saw and experienced of the Scandinavian people they encountered. Artifactual evidence is also available to us, in part because of the particular habit of Vikings to bury their treasure in hoards. We know what their weapons looked like, what materials they were made of, and what weights and balances they had. We know what their armor was made of, and who their opponents were. We can add all of these sources to our reconstruction of Viking combat.

So, while this study is HEMA-adjacent, there are currently no real tournaments or official competitions for Skjoldr or Skeggox in the context in which we wish to apply them. Despite these differences, the pursuit of this knowledge is most certainly a martial art, as our focus is to learn how to most efficiently and quickly do the most physical damage to our opponent, in the historical context and parameters of Viking Age weapon combat.

The art that I will describe in this book is constantly being changed, added to, and learned. I have been hesitant to pin down a snapshot of any particular form during its evolution, but many students have begun to ask for a study reference. Therefore I have decided to put into literary form what has up until now been a purely oral transmission. However, I hope the reader remembers that I am but a humble student of this art, and am continuing to learn with the rest of you, and if you disagree with any of the information put forth in these pages, I welcome you to disprove me in the fighting ring!

Each of the concepts and techniques I will describe here have been demonstrated successfully at fight speed in the ring, by myself or others observed by me, with the weapons I describe. This is not a comprehensive list of every useful action a fighter could take with these weapon sets, as I'm sure we will continue to add knowledge as we move forward in our study, but I hope that this information can at least create a foundation upon which each student can continue to build what suits them.

I will attempt not to repeat descriptions of techniques covered by other HEMA Masters in their currently known treatises. However, because of the nature of biomechanics, and the shape of the weapons we will be discussing, some overlap is inevitable. Some of the techniques I describe have certainly been borrowed from historical fencing manuscripts and then adapted to apply in our context and weapon set.

Unless otherwise specified, the context in which we will work is a duel, a fight between similarly armed opponents, wearing period-accurate attire, but not full battle armor. Imagine the kit that a Scandinavian warrior, advised by Odin to never take more than a few steps from their spear, might be dressed in as they traveled along the open road upon their own peaceful business in the year 800CE. Imagine then that they are set upon by another, similarly attired traveler and a fight to the death ensues.

It would be irresponsible of me to engage in a discussion on how to do terrible physical damage to an opponent without a discussion on personal safety. **Please do not take any chances whatsoever with your physical safety.** Having and using appropriate protective gear is of the utmost importance when engaging in any kind of combat sport, especially one of this nature. Educate yourself, acquire appropriate safety gear, and do not engage in any action that elevates risk to either you or your training partners. I recommend a full kit of HEMA safety gear, as well as full back-of-head protection and thigh protection. Reach out to your local HEMA club if you have questions, or reach out to the greater online HEMA community. I have found the participants of historical combat sports in the US to be generally helpful and genuine in their advice. No one wants anyone else to be seriously injured in the pursuit of this activity. Please be safe. Besides protective gear, weaponry must be safe as well, especially polearms. A blunt steel axe is still a deadly weapon. During the medieval period, the "staff" had the highest recorded kill count of any other weapon in a non-battlefield context. Even a blunt stick can be very dangerous. Thrusting with a shield is very effective at inflicting enormous damage on an opponent. Use safe training weapons if you plan to train with a living partner and want them to stay that way. I am not responsible for any injuries you might incur while engaged in any martial practice.

    Although Viking Age fighters most certainly fought with spears, there is enough other source material from more learned experts than I on the "King of Battle", so I will not attempt to say anything further on that well-covered subject. Neither will I discuss another field of study that has been exhaustively covered by numerous historical Masters throughout medieval European history; single-handed swordplay, except as paired with a Hand Axe or Skjoldr.

This book will be broken into various chapters, which I hope will provide a helpful reference to students who wish to further their study of Dark-Ages weapon-based combat. The first will discuss the Long Axe, or Skeggox. The second concerns the Skjoldr or Round Shield. The third will discuss dual-wielding Hand Axe and Sword. The fourth chapter will cover team combat. The fifth will be a discussion of general concepts and fight geometry. So let us begin.

CHAPTER 1: THE LONG AXE OR SKEGGOX

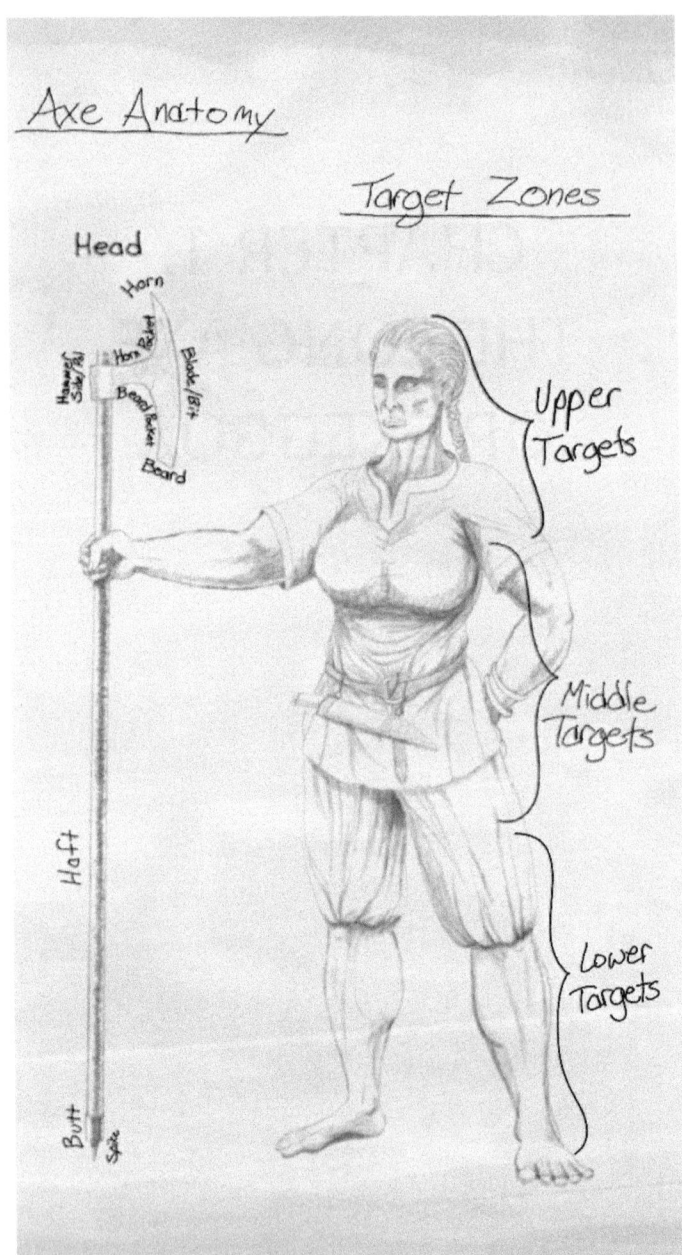

THE ART OF VIKING COMBAT

All positions are referred to by both guard and grip, ie. "Hel's Mast," "Midgard's Prow," etc.

Long Axe Grips

- Asgard
- Midgard
- Hel

Hands transition up & down

Long Axe Guards

- Midgard's Mast
- Asgard's Perch
- Hel's Prow
- Midgard's Oar
- Hel's Anchor
- Hel's Tail

- Hands switch dominant (high) position, axe haft changes sides of the body
- All guards can be done in any of the grip positions or hand placement

Overhand — Strong Defense

Underhand — Strong Offense

Long Axe versus Long Axe

The Long Axe is neither a left-handed nor right-handed weapon. In this section, the hand closest to the axe head will be referred to as the "dominant hand". The Long Axe fighter should learn to switch dominant hands to respond in time to any fight situation. Experimentation will inform the practitioner as to which dominant hand position suits each situation and technique described here. Polearms have the advantage of range over most other weapons besides Spear. They can cut more heavily, breaking through blocks from lesser weapons. The trade-off is speed. The Long Axe is slower than the Spear or the Longsword, in both offense and defense, since the weight of the head(around 3 lbs) is usually at the farthest end from the hands. However, once these characteristics are learned by the fighter, it is one of the most versatile and dangerous weapons in the ring.

The Skeggox can essentially act as three weapons in one; Staff, Axe, and Spear, depending on the situation and how it is wielded. The Skeggox is the ancestor of a large section of the polearm family tree, and has dominated battlefields throughout history. It is the longest-range weapon that will be discussed in this book. There are many other historical treatises on the use of polearms, and biomechanically all of those techniques can be used with almost any polearm. So this section will not serve as a comprehensive log of all possible Long Axe techniques, but will inform some of the basics of the art that may be expanded upon by the student through other sources.

Responding to heavy cuts from above:

1. <u>Oak of Battle</u>: From Midgard's Oar, parry high between your hands with full upward arm extension. Redirect the attack momentum towards your butt-end by lifting your axe head high so the attacker's haft slides down over your non-dominant hand. Simultaneously step offline away from their weapon. Cut or thrust down toward their upper targets.
2. <u>Gut Ripper:</u> From Midgard's Oar, overhand grip, parry high with full upward arm extension between your hands. Push up and forwards. Rotate your axe head low and cut into their middle targets while maintaining bind pressure on their haft. Follow with a step offline and a butt strike to their upper targets.
3. <u>Gungnir's Strike:</u> When you are threatened by thrusts from Hel's Perch, switch to Asgard's Perch, so that your haft extends out in front of you and you are faster than your opponent. Either wait for their attack and displace it offline, followed by closing distance and cutting under to their middle

targets, OR attack first, displacing their axe head offline and striking with your butt to their face or close and cut under to their middle targets. Defend and exit.
4. <u>Asgard's Judgement:</u> When your opponent attacks fast and hard with long cuts and thrusts, take Asgard's Perch, so that your defense is faster. Maintain your butt toward their lower targets, so you may parry off all incoming strikes or thrusts. Transition quickly to Midgard's Mast and cut down fast to their middle or upper targets.

Applying cuts from above:

1. <u>Climbing the Wall:</u> From Hel's Mast, cut down to your opponent's face. If the strike is blocked or parried with the Oar, hook your beard and pull down hard on your opponent's haft, and then thrust into their upper targets. Defend and exit the battle space.
2. <u>Ducking Under:</u> From Hel's Mast, cut down to your opponent's face. When they raise their Oar defense, pull the strike back towards your body by sliding the dominant hand forward as the non-dominant hand draws back, allowing your axe head to drop below their haft. Thrust immediately to their upper or middle targets. Defend and exit the battle space.

Applying cuts from below:
1. <u>Winter's Wind:</u> From Hel's Mast, push both hands straight forward, feinting a high cut from above. Once the opponent lifts their Oar defense, rotate your axe head around low by pulling your dominant hand back and under and pulling your non-dominant hand upward. Step in and apply your cut to their middle targets, keeping your hands high after the strike to maintain your defense as you exit the battle space.
2. <u>The Roof Pole:</u> From Hel's Anchor, bait your upper targets and wait for the strike. Then lift your hands high to block and push forward to cut into their middle or lower targets. If the cut is short, push forward into a thrust, keeping your hands above the axe head to maintain defense.

Defending against cuts from below:
1. <u>The Gate Post:</u> From Asgard's Mast, jam your butt into the ground at an outward angle, while also stepping back the threatened leg. Once the block is complete, step back in again and thrust into their middle or upper targets. Defend and exit.
2. <u>The Ship's Oar:</u> From Midgard's Anchor, jam your horn into the ground at an outward angle, while also stepping back the

threatened leg. Once the block is complete, step back in and cut or thrust into their middle or lower targets. Defend and exit.

Thrusting with the Long Axe:

- *All thrusts should surprise the opponent, and be carried out with hands high and defense in mind, otherwise, you will be left in a fully committed, extended position that is time-consuming to recover from.*
    1. <u>The Viper Strike:</u> From Hel's Prow, pull your axe head back to your side and slide up to Asgard's Prow, hiding your range. The non-dominant hand should grip as far back on the haft as possible. Drop your axe head slightly to feint a low strike. Once your opponent's face is no longer defended, shoot your axe head forward at their upper targets by sliding your dominant hand backward to meet the other hand, and then sliding the non-dominant hand back down the haft as well, sending the thrust out to full range. Once complete, defend and exit.
    2. <u>The Lion's Paw:</u> From Midgard's Oar, wait for your opponent to take a long Prow guard. Displace their defense by slapping their axe head offline, and immediately thrust to their face, placing your haft to defend against a return cut. Exit fight range.

Responding to Thrusts:

3. <u>Valkyrie's Vengeance:</u> When you are waiting just outside the opponent's single-hand thrust range, and have baited yourself by moving into Hel's Tail, and your opponent tries a long thrust to your middle or upper targets, step sideways and forward offline towards your non-dominant hand, turning your shoulders perpendicular to your opponent. Parry the haft of their incoming strike with your dominant hand. Send a single-handed non-dominant thrust at your opponent's upper targets. Continue to step around and away to exit fight range.
4. <u>The Ram Charge:</u> When your opponent thrusts from a low position, meet it with your own thrust. Target their axe head so that both axes bind in the horn pocket. Push forward and towards your dominant hand side, scooping your horn under their beard. Push their axe head high and step in, maintaining the bind, and bring your butt around to strike their upper targets, or attempt a Collar Throw.

Grappling and Manipulation with the Long Axe:

- *Hooking with the Beard and trapping with the horn should be applied to the opponent's weapons and limbs whenever possible. Always carry a dagger. It is sometimes useful to grip it in the non-dominant hand against the axe haft.*

This will impede grip switching but will provide an immediate attack option at close range where the Long Axe is less efficient.

1. <u>Collar Throw:</u> This technique is shown in Hans Talhoffer's treatise. When you meet your opponent in an equal high bind, both with axe heads high in Midgard's Mast, step quickly behind their leading leg so that your non-dominant side hip is behind theirs. Simultaneously, wind your haft around theirs so that your butt end crosses their throat. Twist your torso and throw them backward across your hip.

2. <u>The Grave Digger:</u> When responding to a high cut at closer range, parry in Midgard's Anchor. Instead of cutting, reach your axe head forward and hook behind their leading knee. Pull upwards to raise their foot off the ground, and push your haft across their body, trapping their arms and forcing them to fall backward. If they try to hop back and don't fall, hook a toe behind the hopping foot. Beware of daggers.

CHAPTER 2: THE VIKING SHIELD, OR SKJOLDR

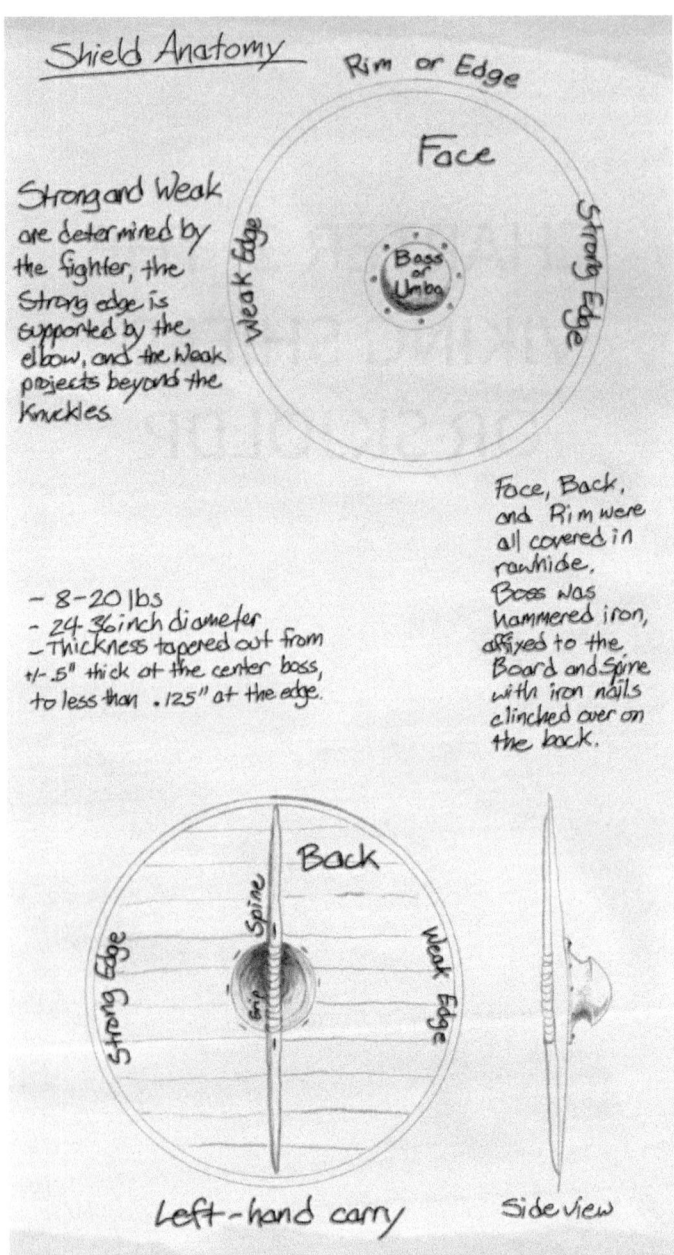

Shield versus Shield, Right Hand Dominant

*The Skjoldr is an iron-bossed, wood-plank constructed, center-grip round shield, held in the fighter's naturally **non-dominant** hand. Historically, it displayed a wide range of sizes and weights, presumably to the specifications and physical size of each individual fighter. Some shields we have found are heavily battle-scarred and repaired and obviously saw use in many fights. We also have evidence of heavily gilded intricately ornamented shields that would have been unwieldy on the battlefield or dueling grounds but were buried with important individuals to denote their status. Aside from ornamentation, all of these shields share the same characteristics, and this shape was continually used up into the early medieval period, finding its final form as the Buckler of the Tower Ms., AKA I.33, in the 14th century.*

When doing any work with the Skjoldr, it is important to remember that it is the primary weapon; the largest object in the battle space. It will not only protect you, it will also create an opening for you to apply your bladed weapon into, but only if you can train up to wield it correctly. It is also crucial to remember to train safely with your partner, given that the Skjoldr is such a devastating bludgeoning weapon.

The Skjoldr is naturally divided in half along the spine, and I refer to the strong edge or weak edge not to indicate better or worse, but for the sake of understanding which part of the weapon we're discussing. This property is similar to the division of strong and weak on a sword blade; a property of physics and an artifact of the center grip. A center-grip shield of any shape may be pivoted in the opponent's hand by applying some kind of pressure to the weak edge. This is called "Opening the Door", and allows a blade to enter and strike a target zone.

Most of the techniques given here can be done with either a Viking Sword or Hand Axe to accompany the Skjoldr, and will be indicated if only one or the other applies. I will not discuss any other accompanying weapons such as spear or dagger, as both of these weapons have been covered extensively elsewhere. Since the Skjoldr does not switch sides like the Skeggox, these techniques will only apply against an opponent that uses the same shield arm.

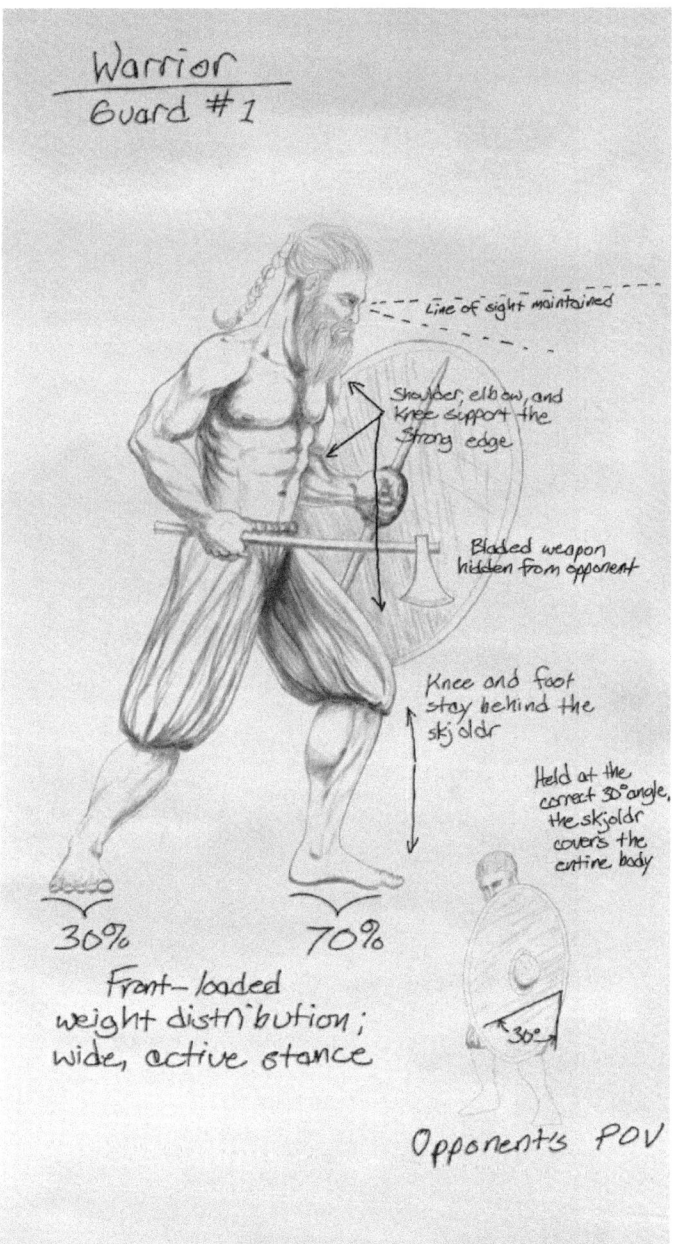

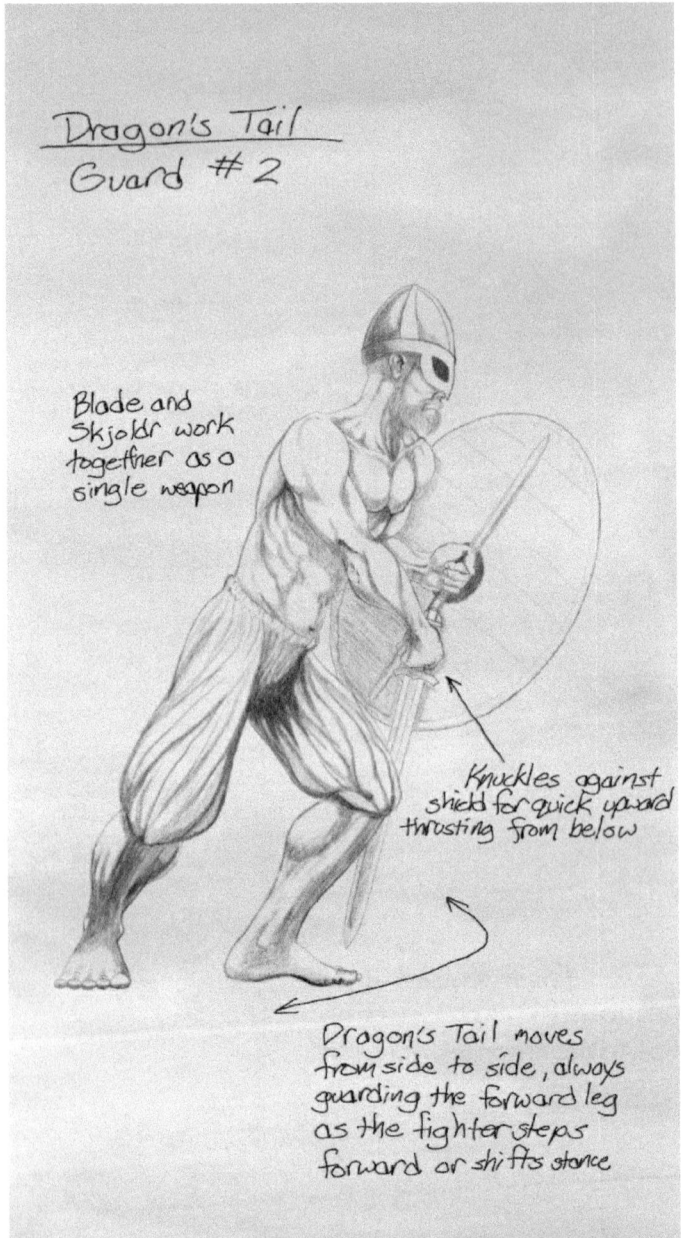

Dragon's Head
Guard #3

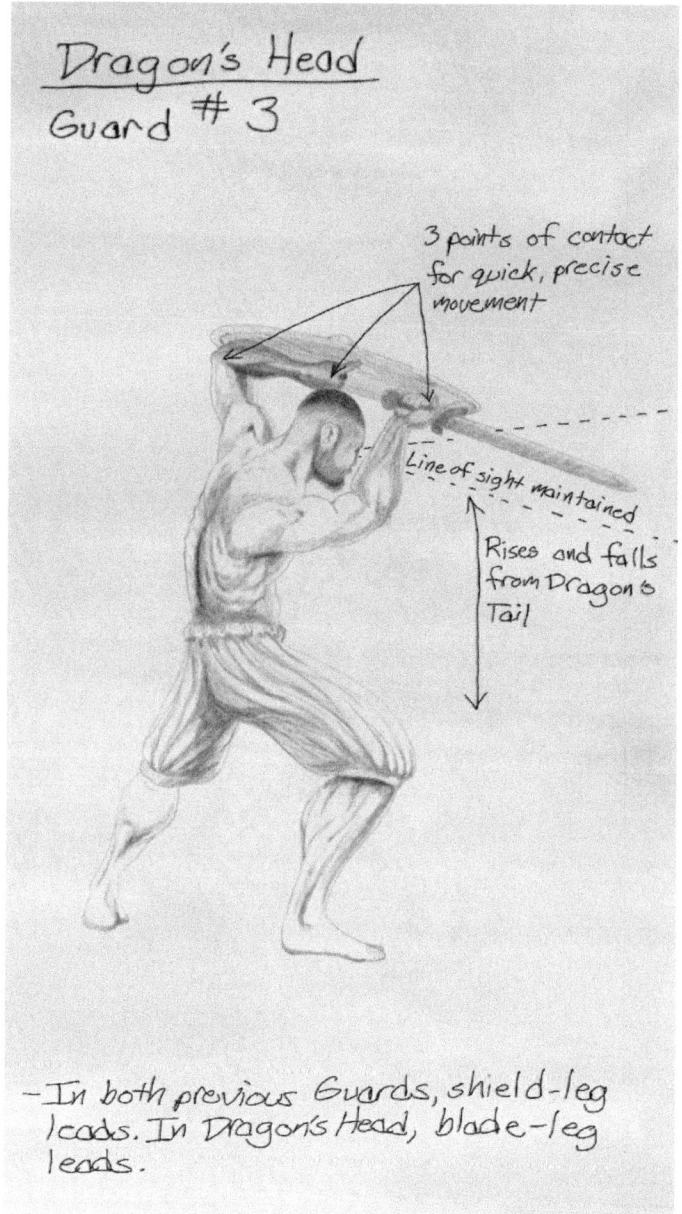

3 points of contact for quick, precise movement

Line of sight maintained

Rises and falls from Dragon's Tail

— In both previous Guards, shield-leg leads. In Dragon's Head, blade-leg leads.

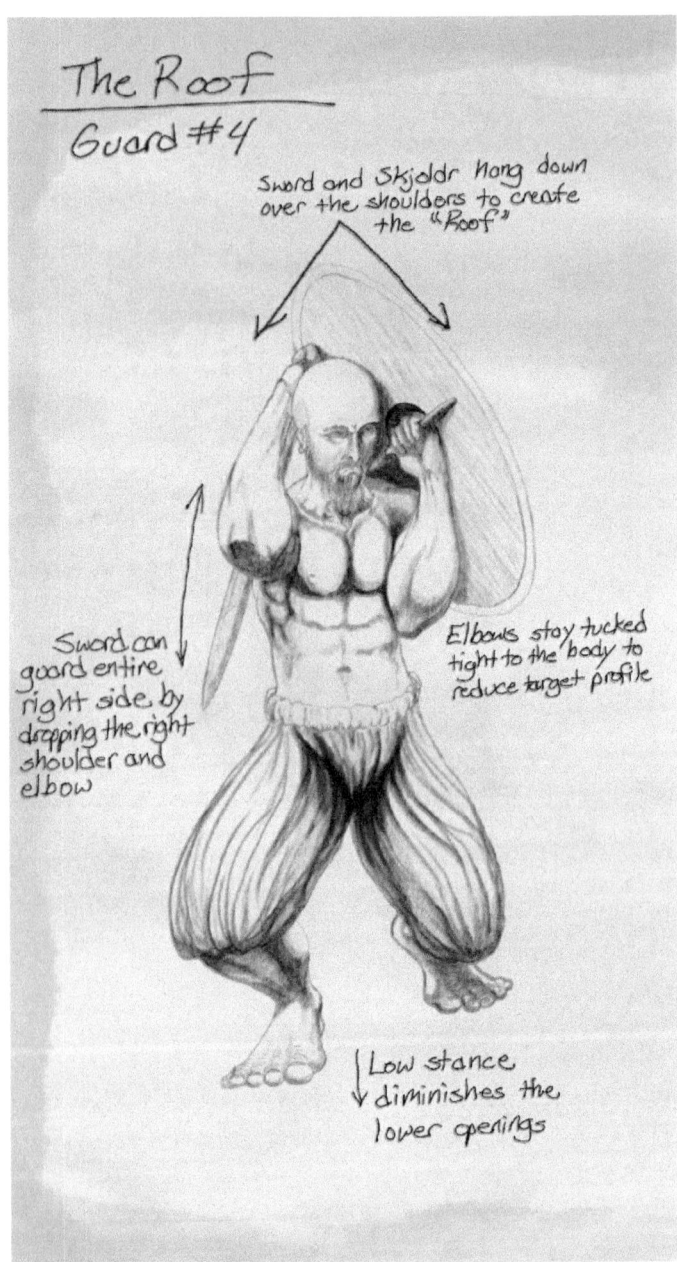

General Application:
1. The Skjoldr and accompanying bladed weapon exist as a single weapon system. Strikes should be done with both simultaneously, using the shield as an active component of every attack. An alternating tempo of striking with the blade and then parrying with the shield fight rhythm is very predictable and will get you killed because it only applies half of your weapon system at a time. However, this is not to say that the shield and blade should both strike to the same target. It is usually advantageous to strike toward opposing diagonal targets, splitting the opponent's focus on defense.
2. When thrusting with the Skjoldr, the boss should not be the striking face. This only extends your reach by about half an inch or so and is a "push" not a thrust, only useful for creating space between you and your opponent. All thrusts should be done with the weak edge. This adds about 15 inches to the range of your strike, and also provides options to control your opponent's weapons and body, as will be discussed later.
3. A shield-bearer is generally the shortest-range fighter in the ring. This means that there cannot be any retreat. The shield

fighter must continually push forward through the range of their opponent to enter their own striking range. But that is the beauty of a shield; it covers you, it becomes your fortress, and you live behind that wall. Anything in front of it dies, including any part of you that extends beyond the safety of your wall, so do not overreach it or step in front of it. The Skjoldr moves forward and takes battle space, and the fighter follows behind, repeating until victory is achieved.

4. Unless you are standing in a Skjoldlina, the shield should never be held flat in front of you. You must maintain control of the axis on which it rotates (the grip), and prevent your opponent from "opening the door" and completing an attack. The skjoldr should lay across the back of your forearm so that it projects at an approximate 30-degree angle, and blows from your opponent glance off of it rather than impact.

Attacks:

- *To complete an attack on your opponent, their shield must be moved from its defensive position. This can be achieved in one of two ways; you must either physically move their shield out of the way, or you must convince them to move it.*

1. <u>The Wolf Attack:</u> Feint a high dominant-side strike with your blade so that your opponent lifts their shield. Redirect to cut at their lower targets. When they drop shield to parry, quickly wind upward again with the back edge of your blade toward their upper targets over the top of their shield. When they raise shield to block this, sweep your shield across toward your blade, trapping their weapons, and simultaneously swing your blade around overhead to strike their dominant-side upper targets.
2. <u>The Bear attack:</u> This technique works best with a hand axe. When you are fighting close and have trapped your opponent toward their blade but are unable to apply a cut, hook with your axe low behind their forward leg. Pull with your axe and push forward with your skjoldr into their chest, so that they fall backward. If they resist and hop backward to escape, pull the hooked knee outward and sideways to twist them off balance and put them down.
3. <u>The Dragon's Bite:</u> When you stand in Dragon's Head and your opponent thrusts or cuts from below towards your middle targets, drop the skjoldr down towards Dragon's Tail in front of you so that you catch their weapon on the right side intersection of your weapons. Parry the

attack away across your dominant side. Pressing in, trap their weapons on their shield side. While maintaining the trap, roll your weak edge counter-clockwise toward them with the blade following, so that it rotates around in line for a thrust to their face. Your blade arm should cross over the top of your shield arm. Step to your non-dominant side as you strike.

4. <u>The Skull Cleaver:</u> This technique works best with a sword. This cut removes the top rear non-dominant side quarter of the opponent's skull, as is shown in archeological finds. When you have trapped your opponent's skjoldr towards their blade, step around your skjoldr towards their non-dominant side. Cut upwards to their upper target with the short edge of your sword or blade of your axe. In sparring, target your opponent's shoulder rather than the back of their head. Safety first.

5. <u>The Key Thrust:</u> Best executed from Warrior Guard or Roof Guard. When your opponent is moving between actions, and has slightly opened their door, brace your sword edge on the weak edge of your shield with your fingernails to the sky. The flat of the sword is too flexible for this. Push the sword tip toward them with the shield to contact the weak edge of their shield.

Then, forcing your hands together, use the leverage of the skjoldr to pry open their door. Use the weight of the skjoldr to drive a thrust into their middle targets.

6. <u>The Wrist Cutter:</u> Best executed from Warrior Guard. Before you enter strike range, drop your blade tip towards your dominant side, feinting an outside overhand cut. When your opponent opens their shield to deflect the strike so you can see their belt buckle, whip your blade around over inside and cut their shield wrist as you step left and block their blade with your shield. If you cannot strike their wrist, attack the target most accessible to your blade with a cut or thrust.

Binds and Manipulation:

- *The Skjoldr is large and in charge. It commands the most mass in the battle space, and therefore, the most momentum. It can push and pull, moving your opponent's weapons and body where you want them.*

    1. <u>The Door Buster:</u> When you feel safe from low attacks because your opponent holds their weapon high, engage a weak edge shield bind. Lift your bottom edge so as to present your shield face to the sky. Push forward and roll your edge across to open the strong edge of their shield, while also trapping both of their weapons toward

their dominant side. This will allow an opening for your blade to thrust into their middle targets, with an option for a shield thrust to their face.

2. <u>The Shoulder Trap:</u> Thrust with your skjoldr into your opponent's blade-side shoulder. Maintain contact, so that their blade arm cannot strike over your shield. Feint high and cut low to their leg with a sword, or hook your axe behind their knee and execute the Bear Attack. Beware of shield thrusts to your face. If their shield wrist is exposed, target that immediately, followed by a thrust or cut to their body or head.

3. <u>The Arm Breaker:</u> When your opponent hooks the top weak edge of your shield with a hand axe to pull it down, hook your axe over theirs, trapping it on your shield rim. Roll your shield towards the weak edge, maintaining their axe on your shield edge, and step back wide with your dominant-side leg, spinning and pulling down, so that your shield elbow is next to their blade elbow, and your shield shoulder is next to their blade shoulder. This technique should be used very carefully, because it applies a full arm-bar.

<u>Shield versus Long Axe</u>

General Application:

A Skjoldr fighter is disadvantaged in range but advantaged in defense, the opposite being true for the Long Axe fighter. Additional weapons can fill the gaps in offense and defense. A skjoldr fighter might throw their hand axe to compensate for their lack of range, so long as they have a sword or seax to draw as they close distance. A Skeggox fighter might grip a seax or hand axe in their non-dominant hand for close-range encounters. Conversely, range can be changed to advantage one fighter or the other. When feeling too pressed, a Skeggox fighter might step back or around their opponent to relieve the pressure and gain the upper hand. A Skjoldr fighter who feels too short on range must press in where their blade can work.

From the Axe:

- *It is generally advantageous for the Skeggox fighter to switch dominant hands when facing a skjoldr fighter, so that the axe head can address the opponent's blade side, requiring them to parry with their blade or cross their arms. Knowing they must close, the Skeggox must outmaneuver them. An overhand grip is often advantageous against the mass of a skjoldr.*
    1. <u>Climbing the Wall:</u> This technique can be adapted directly to a Sjkoldr opponent. Once the hook has been applied to the rim, step around to their skjoldr side as you thrust into their upper target. This side step

will keep you safe from their blade if your thrust misses.
2. Winter's Wind: If your thrust is unsuccessful, immediately transition to Winter's Wind, and cut quickly to their forward leg.
3. If this cut is unsuccessful, parry off the incoming blade strike with Midgard's Anchor, and then immediately send your butt into their teeth or ear. Switch to Asgard's Mast, and cut quickly to their upper targets.

From the Skjoldr (Right-hand Dominant):

- *It is important for a skjoldr fighter to be very defensive until they are able to press inside the Skeggox's range. Long-range thrusts can be dangerous both over and under the skjoldr, so a wider stance is advisable. At no time should a skjoldr fighter ever retreat or step backward, for this only removes them from their own range and puts them at the opponent's. There is no retreat needed when you are safe behind the wall of your shield.*
    1. WolfBear: When the Skeggox fighter strikes down from above to cut or hook, raise the skjoldr high and press in, applying the Wolf Attack or the Bear Attack.
    2. Arm Breaker: If the axe makes a hook on the rim, roll it off and apply the Arm Breaker,

with a cut following.
- If rolling toward the Strong of your Skjoldr, push forward and trap their haft against their body. Step to your right and cut to any opening.
- If rolling toward the Weak of your Skjoldr, maintain their hook on your rim and drive their horn into the ground, thrusting over top of the skjoldr into their upper openings.
3. <u>The Raven's Wing:</u> Approach the opponent in Dragon's Tail, baiting a high thrust to your face above the shield. When they take the bait, sweep their attack away with the skjoldr and thrust upwards into their middle targets. Defend and exit their range.

CHAPTER 3: DUAL WEILDING HAND AXE AND SWORD

It could be assumed that anyone in the Dark Ages who could afford to have a master bladesmith craft them the bloodsnake might not be able to afford another sword, but could certainly afford a hand axe. Biomechanically, this combination is similar to both sword/buckler and sword/parrying dagger, combining aspects of each of these non-dominant hand weapons to accompany the sword. Two variations have become apparent: sword-dominant or axe-dominant. Both have their advantages and drawbacks. Regardless of which is held in the dominant hand, there are two guards; the Skeggox and the Scorpion.

THE ART OF VIKING COMBAT

The Skeggox

- Axe Dominant: The sword is used for deflection and parrying, allowing the axe to break away and cut in hard. This position is also great for hooking and manipulating the opponent's weapon, accompanied by a quick thrust from the sword.
- Sword Dominant: The sword is supported by the axe for an extra strong parrying stance. It uses the axe as a point of leverage, creating much stronger bind geometry, and adding momentum to any thrust.
- An obvious drawback to this guard is that both weapons may be trapped together, so the dual wielder must remain nimble and quick-eyed.

The Scorpion

- Axe Dominant: Range is seemingly reduced, baiting the opponent to step in. When they attack, parry and hook with the axe, accompanied by a sword thrust, stepping offline.
- Sword Dominant: Long-range position, allowing for precise swordplay, interspersed with heavy strikes from the axe.
- The Scorpion provides both Long-Range defense and the threat of a heavy strike always imminent. Having the choice of both offense and defense in either hand is always

advantageous, as long as one remembers to use both accordingly.

Both of these guards may be used when wielding dual swords or dual axes, as well. Other more knowledgeable sources have treated dual sword wielding at great length, and I have nothing more to add to that body of work. I will, however, say a few words on dual-wielding axes.

Beard and Horn shape is integral to choosing a good pair of hand axes. I advise a longer Horn and more shallow Beard for the dominant hand, giving precedence to quick cuts and thrusts, whereas a shallower Horn and longer Beard are more suited to the non-dominant hand for weapon trapping and parrying. Dual-wielding hand axes make you the shortest-range fighter on the field. There is an option to throw one from longer range, requiring you to draw another weapon or go without. However, as you enter the battle space, you must be extremely fast in both footwork and reflexes, and either parry and close, or immediately rush in. Dual-wielding axes is not easy.

Sword Anatomy

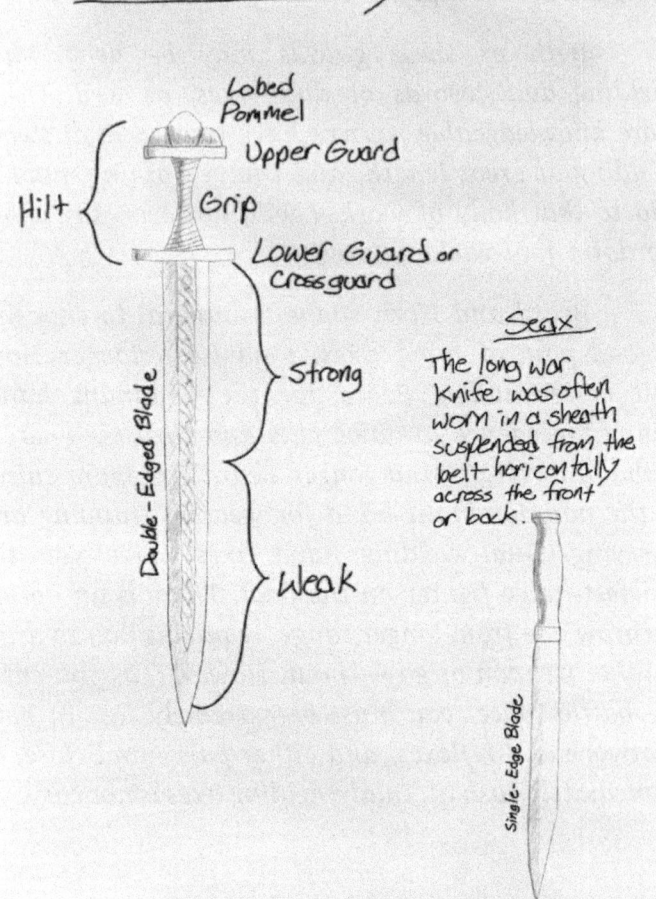

Seax

The long war knife was often worn in a sheath suspended from the belt horizontally across the front or back.

+/- 4" Grip
Pattern welded steel alloy blade with iron furniture. The ancient Scandinavian people traded for steel smelting techniques in the Middle East, and dominated the battlefield with superior sword technology, bending and even cutting through the blades of their opponents. Blades of vanquished foes were often ritually destroyed and or buried, rather than recycled or re-used.

Laxdaela Saga Ch. LVII as translated by Murial A.C. Press

"...But what I wish is this, that you would lend me the sword Skofnung, for then I ween I shall be able to overcome a mere renegade, be he ever so mighty a man with his hands. 'You must have your way in this', said Eid, 'but it will not come to me unawares, if, someday, you should come to rue this willfulness. But inasmuch as you will have it that you are doing this for my sake, what you ask for will not be withheld for I think Skofnung well bestowed if you bear it. But the nature of the sword is such that the sun must not shine upon its hilt, nor must it be drawn if a woman should be near. If a man be wounded by the sword the hurt may not be healed, unless by the healing stone that goes with the sword be rubbed thereon."

- I would postulate that the tri-lobed shape of the pommel of a Viking Sword originated as the accompanying "Healing Stone", bound in a small pouch with cord or wire to the Upper Guard. The ancient Scandinavian fighters were pragmatic folk, and it makes sense to attach the required stone in a way that is furthest from the end that causes the incurable cut, but also still immediately at hand. This could also allow for adjustable balance of the weapon, by adding or subtracting sand or stones.

CHAPTER 4: TEAM COMBAT

There are so many mentions of two friends, a few brothers, or some other team forming in the Sagas and cooperatively battling numerous foes. Obviously, the possible combinations of fighters and weapon sets are too numerous to discuss all scenarios. Therefore, specific techniques will not be discussed in detail, rather we will look at general concepts, strategies, and formations. From here on we will assume the Fight Team is comprised of two fighters. At first glance, this idea lends itself to two basic formations, which any pair of untrained people will revert to when threatened. These are:

So as we look at our two formations again, we can see that certain weapon pairings are more or less suited to each. Obviously, two skjoldr fighters will be more effective in the Side by Side formation as a Skjoldlina. A long axe or spear fighter will do well to tuck up behind a skjoldr fighter in the Front and Back formation. Let's explore these concepts a bit more in-depth.

Side by Side:

- This is a very versatile, attack-focused formation. Both fighters face the enemy at equal distance and therefore have equal chance to attack or be attacked. They can watch out for and defend eachother. They can stay together, or split up and surround the opponent. It is easy for these two fighters to stay in step and use non-verbal communication to move around the battlefield as a single unit. This is the beginning of the classic shield wall that has been employed by shield fight teams throughout history and across cultures.
- A modified Side by Side formation is the Break. Fighters break physical contact to try and surround the enemy. This is especially effective in a two-versus-one situation, as well as when terrain features like rocks or trees provide static cover.

Front and Back:

- This is a very defensive, tactical formation. The front fighter has an equal chance of being attacked by all opponents in front of them, but that leaves the back fighter free to apply attacks and techniques that might be too dangerous or impossible while also trying to defend themselves. Therefore, the back fighter needs a long-range weapon, and the front fighter must be very defensive. This formation naturally encourages a front-low back-high stance, giving the most defense to the lower openings and creating attack space over the front fighter's head or shoulders for the back fighter to apply into.

- A modified Front and Back formation is Back to Back. If the fight team is facing a larger force, or if the enemy has broken formation and surrounded them, they must face all incoming attacks without losing physical contact and non-verbal communication with their partner.

These two primary formations may be moved in and out of, depending on the nature of the fight. A Back to Back formation can quickly turn into Side by Side if lateral pressure is applied, and vice versa. A Side by Side may become Front and Back by allowing one fighter to press as the other steps in behind them. A fight team should be able to transition smoothly from one formation to the next as the situation requires, communicating with their partner as they move.

In the chaos of battle, with sweat in your eyes and shield thunder in your ears, it is easy to get tunnel vision. It is of utmost importance to not slay your own battle buddy. Be aware of them. Practice non-verbal communication. Use body contact to convey your position to the other. Vocal signals are important as well, but they must be clear and direct. Just yelling "Watch out!" is not communication, it is a distraction. Give specific instructions, and let your partner know what you are doing before you do it. Surprise the enemy, not your friend.

CHAPTER 5: FIGHT STRATEGY AND BATTLE GEOMETRY

I always tell my students that weapon combat is 80% in the mind. Once a person can understand the concepts of strategy, and think through the spatial geometry of each conflict, their body will follow right along behind.

Strategy

In any fight, no matter its scope or context, there are very specific goals each fighter must achieve. First and foremost of these goals is of course, "victory". However, achieving "victory" can be more nebulous than first glance will reveal. For all fighters to recognize who the victor is, there must be context, rules, parameters; requirements that must be met. In some cases, the rules are clear and strict, and understood by all. They are enforced by some governing body. In other cases, the parameters are a looser set of cultural mores, enforced through societal pressure. In some contexts, the rules are no rules, and the victor is the one who lives the longest. Knowing which of these contexts you are fighting under is key to understanding and creating a fight strategy. However, some concepts can be applied universally in any context.

Intensity is key in any fight and should be modulated according to the parameters for victory. Intensity should not be mistaken for Speed, or vice versa, although that is one of the elements Intensity requires. Timing is integral to the equation, as well as Range. The final element of Intensity is Power. Power must be carefully controlled; too much may over-extend a strike or injure a sparring partner. Too little may not push through a guard or parry a strike.

In cases where the victory parameter is death, Intensity must be at its peak. Both J. Lichtenauer, who told us to "Take the Vor", and Kobra Kai dojo, which advises to "Strike first, strike hard, show no mercy", understood Intensity to be the primary requirement for a swift victory.

Speed of action, **Timing** of action, and awareness of the **Range** of both fighters are the basic elements that must be combined appropriately to apply the correct **Power**, and thereby modulate **Intensity**.

Speed:

At first glance, Speed seems very simply understood, but as we look more closely, details emerge. We could say that Speed is the rate at which a fighter moves. It includes dancing a circle around an opponent, as well as twitching a parry an inch into place. Any action a fighter takes must have the appropriate rate of Speed applied. Speed may be slow or fast, depending on the requirements of the situation.

Timing:

Speed is wasted without the correct application of Timing, which is the choice a fighter makes as to when to take any given action. Timing must be proactive and reactive to provide the most benefit. A fighter must be able to both attack and defend at the correct time to claim victory.

Range:

The knowledge of your own Range can be collected for any weapon set with enough practice. But an opponent's Range must be guessed until the fight has progressed enough for it to be revealed, and Range can be easily masked. Therefore, it can be advantageous for unseasoned fighters to understand how to watch for the tells that reveal range. Slow recovery from a strike can indicate the opponent has fully committed to their full range. An opponent's Range should be tested very carefully, and even more so when they wield a polearm. If they are less experienced and unaware of their own Range, they will likely strike too soon, falling short and exposing their own Range simultaneously. This is the magic moment, just after their short strike, before they have recovered. It is natural to backstep safely out of the Battle Space here. Do not. Press forward and provide a quick series of strikes to diagonally opposed targets. However, if the opponent is more experienced, they will hide their Range until you are within it, and then strike. Quick defense here is key, allowing your opponent to teach you their Range. Feints are useful, not only of the weapon, but the feet, shoulders, and eyes as well.

Power:

Once these other elements are understood, the question of how much power should be applied to any given action can be answered. The fight parameters and context must be considered as well, and Power modulated for lethality. Power must be enough to carry a fighter through Range, at the correct Timing, to provide the necessary Speed, but with enough control to be able to respond to the next action without overextending.

Battle Space Geometry

*The **Battle Space** is the area between two fighters where the fighter with the longest Range may come into contact with their opponent by taking a single action, such as a thrust with a passing step.*

- All combat can be broken down to geometry and timing, especially weapon combat. Swords, polearms, and shields become lines, points, and planes, and timing and range determine how they interact around eachother.
- Crossing elements parry, while parallel elements strike. This means that if a line crosses a plane or another line in the Battle Space, the strike is impeded. But if a point passes parallel to a plane, or lines pass parallel to eachother, the strike is successful.

So then, in any combative action, great focus should be aimed at staying aware and making use of this universal geometric concept, regardless of the weapon set or technique being applied. This is the truest essence of any weapon combat.

The size of the Battle Space is always determined by the longest-range weapon.

Therefore, the shorter-ranged fighter must enter the space defensively, and cross into their own range as quickly as possible.

Point, Line, and Plane:

The geometric element "Point" is represented by a thrust. It is the tip of any bladed weapon that is intended to pierce a target. The "Line" is any axe haft or sword blade. A "Plane" is the shield, in any of its forms and shapes. At speed, the chance of blocking the Point of a thrust with the Line of a sword blade is almost zero. So then the only parrying option is to engage the Line of our haft or blade with the line that exists behind the Point. However, this creates a dynamic where the Point has already passed inside our guard and has a very real chance of penetrating our targets. Planes provide wide areas of protection from both Lines and Points, but are by very nature unable to work a cut or a thrust into a small opening that a Point could enter. As we attack with a Point, we must always consider the angle of the Line of our attack, so that it may pass parallel to the Plane of a shield or the Line of a parry. Wrist rotations may be required to adjust biomechanically to the geometric impediment to our target.

In Conclusion:

The art described here has been practiced earnestly and with the true intention of discovering what could have been possible. I have added a final section for the recording of your own observations and conclusions, I hope you interact with this work in whatever way most suites your pursuit of this knowledge. We practice a living and evolving art, and the truth of every technique is always discovered at speed, in the ring. See you there.

I hope that this book will serve well in the practice room. I have left several pages here for the practitioner to add their own notes and illustrations.

M.J. ERBACH

THE ART OF VIKING COMBAT

M.J. ERBACH

THE ART OF VIKING COMBAT

THE ART OF VIKING COMBAT

M.J. ERBACH

ABOUT THE AUTHOR

M. J. Erbach

Mike "the Viking" Erbach has been fascinated by all things "Viking" since his first exposure to runes as a child reading "The Hobbit". He is a US Army combat veteran, and has been studying martial arts since 2005. His obsession with Viking Combat reconstruction has been a journey of ten years so far, fascilitated through Warriors of Ash, the HEMA school of which he is a founding member. All proceeds from the sale of this book go to support that non-profit educational organization.

BOOKS BY THIS AUTHOR

Shee, The Cannibals' Last Child

Shee struggles across the barren wastes of an unrecognizable Urth in the far distant future, gaining friends and finding the true meaning of family in creatures both monstrous and human. She escapes the horror she grew up under and sets out to discover her own power, create her own destiny, and battle all enemies that threaten the existence of those she loves.

Made in the USA
Las Vegas, NV
04 April 2025